KNOCK KNOCK! AGAIN

The New BIGGEST Best Joke Book EVER

Highlights Press
Honesdale, Pennsylvania

Contributing Illustrators: Hector Borlasca, Forrest Burdett,
Dave Clegg, David Coulson, Russ Cox, Jef Czekaj, Mike Dammer,
Jack Desrocher, Valerio Fabbretti, Keith Frawley, Patrick Girouard,
Bill Golliher, Kelly Kennedy, Sue King, Dave Klug, Genevieve Kote,
Rita Lascaro, Pat Lewis, Lyn Martin, Erin Mauterer, Mike Moran,
Scott Nickel, Neil Numberman, Bob Ostrom, Jim Paillot, Rich Powell,
Kevin Rechin, Cole Roberts, Rico Schacherl, Luke Seguin-Magee,
Vahan Shirvanian, Erica Sirotich, Jim Steck, Karen Stormer Brooks,
Rick Stromoski, Bob Vojtko, Pete Whitehead, Kevin Zimmer

For information about permission to reprint selections from this book,
please contact permissions@highlights.com.

Published by Highlights Press
815 Church Street
Honesdale, Pennsylvania 18431

ISBN: 978-1-64472-451-4
Manufactured in Minster, OH, USA
Mfg. 03/2022

First edition
Visit our website at Highlights.com.

10 9 8 7 6 5

Contents

Animal Antics

Knock, knock.

Who's there?
Rhino.
Rhino who?
Rhino these knock-knock jokes
are going to make you laugh.

Knock, knock.
Who's there?
Aardvark.
Aardvark who?
Aardvark a hundred miles
for one of your smiles!

Knock, knock.

Who's there?

Sheep.

Sheep who?

Sheep-ers! Don't you recognize me?

Knock, knock.

Who's there?

Badge.

Badge who?

I hate to badger you, but can you let me in?

Knock, knock.
Who's there?
Chimp.
Chimp who?
I think you mean
to say *shampoo.*

Knock, knock.
Who's there?
A parrot.
A parrot who?
A-parrot-ly I'm at the wrong door.

Knock, knock.
Who's there?
Terry.
Terry who?
It's Terry-fying to come
face-to-face with a bear!

Knock, knock.
Who's there?
Quack.
Quack *who?*
I was up at the *quack* of dawn.

Knock, knock.
Who's there?
Alibi.
Alibi who?
Alibi the dog
a birthday treat.

Knock, knock.
Who's there?
Fission.
Fission who?
Fission a bowl are safe from the cat.

Knock, knock.
Who's there?
Arthur.
Arthur who?
Arthur any cats in your house?

Knock, knock.
Who's there?
Bark.
Bark who?
Bark your car in the driveway.

Knock, knock.
Who's there?
Beak.
Beak who?
Beak careful crossing
the street!

Knock, knock.

Who's there?
Bunny.
Bunny who?
Bunny thing is, I've forgotten!

Knock, knock.
Who's there?
Foal.
Foal who?
Foal the last time, let me in!

Knock, knock.
Who's there?
Calf.
Calf who?
I calf to finish my homework.

Knock, knock.
Who's there?
Camel.
Camel who?
Camel little closer—I have a secret to tell you.

Knock, knock.
Who's there?
Caribou.
Caribou who?
I caribou-t you a lot!

Knock, knock.
Who's there?
Deer.
Deer who?
Deer to be different!

Knock, knock.
Who's there?
Claw.
Claw who?
Stop in the name of the claw!

Knock, knock.
Who's there?
Cats go.
Cats go who?
No, cats go *meow!*

Knock, knock.
Who's there?
Fiona.
Fiona who?
Fiona lookout for snakes!

Knock, knock.
Who's there?
Census.
Census who?
Census Saturday, let's go to the zoo.

Knock, knock.
Who's there?
Chicken.
Chicken who?
Just chicken on you to make sure you're okay.

Knock, knock.
Who's there?
Goat.
Goat who?
Goat to lunch with me!

Knock, knock.
Who's there?
Wander.
Wander who?
I wander pet those cute kittens.

Knock, knock.
Who's there?
Rosa.
Rosa who?
Sharks have sharp Rosa teeth—be careful!

Knock, knock.

Who's there?

Bat.

Bat who?

Bat you've never heard
this knock-knock joke!

Knock, knock.

Who's there?

Tuna.

Tuna who?

Tuna the lights on. I can't see a thing!

Knock, knock.

Who's there?

Cat.

Cat who?

Cat you just let me in?

Knock, knock.

Who's there?

Dove.

Dove who?

I'd dove to stay, but I have to go!

Knock, knock.
Who's there?
Dragon.
Dragon who?
You're dragon your feet again.

Knock, knock.
Who's there?
Adeline.
Adeline who?
You should Adeline to your drawing
of a unicorn.

Knock, knock.
Who's there?
Fido.
Fido who?
Fido known you were sick, I would have brought soup.

Knock, knock.

Who's there?

Adele.

Adele who?

Adele-phant who is lost.

Knock, knock.

Who's there?

Cows.

Cows who?

Cows say "moo," not "who."

Knock, knock.
Who's there?
Cadillac.
Cadillac who?
Cadillacs to be pet behind its ears.

Knock, knock.
Who's there?
Fur.
Fur who?
Waiting fur you to open the door.

Knock, knock.
Who's there?
Wolf pack.
Wolf pack who?
Wolf pack some food and go on a picnic.

Knock, knock.
Who's there?
Bob.
Bob who?
Bobcats are named for their short tails.

Knock, knock.
Who's there?
Gibbon.
Gibbon who?
Gibbon my dog a bath.

Knock, knock.
Who's there?
Giraffe.
Giraffe who?
Sorry I'm late. I was stuck in a giraffe-ic jam.

Knock, knock.
Who's there?
Impatient cow.
Impatient c—
MOO!

Knock, knock.
Who's there?
Gnu.
Gnu who?
Gnu you'd ask me that.

Knock, knock.
Who's there?
Goose.
Goose who?
No, you goose who!

Knock, knock.
Who's there?
Hare.
Hare who?
Hare you are!

Knock, knock.
Who's there?
Hawk.
Hawk who?
Well, this is hawk-ward. Don't you remember me?

Knock, knock.
Who's there?
Thomas.
Thomas who?
That hippopo-Thomas is big!

Knock, knock.
Who's there?
Jim.
Jim who?
Jim-panzees are different from apes.

Knock, knock.
Who's there?
Indy.
Indy who?
Indy rainforest lives a monkey.

Knock, knock.
Who's there?
Yak.
Yak who?
Yak-tually, I was just leaving.

Knock, knock.
Who's there?
Juicy.
Juicy who?
Juicy the big polar bear?

Knock, knock.
Who's there?
Kitten.
Kitten who?
I'm just kitten with you!

Knock, knock.
Who's there?
Lion.
Lion who?
Lion on your doorstep. Open up!

Knock, knock.
Who's there?
Macaw.
Macaw who?
Macaw has a flat tire—can you help?

Knock, knock.
Who's there?
Hugh.
Hugh who?
Whales are Hugh-mongous!

Knock, knock.

Who's there?

Koala.

Koala who?

These are some koala-ty knock-knock jokes!

Knock, knock.

Who's there?

Mane.

Mane who?

Mane to tell you I was stopping by.

Knock, knock.
Who's there?
Liza Little.
Liza Little who?
I know I Liza Little, but I did see a bear!

Knock, knock.
Who's there?
Whitcomb.
Whitcomb who?
Whitcomb first, the chicken or the egg?

Knock, knock.
Who's there?
Minnow.
Minnow who?
Let minnow if you figure it out!

Knock, knock.
Who's there?
Moo.
Moo *who?*
Happy *Moo* Year!

Knock, knock.
Who's there?
Parrot.
Parrot who?
Parrot who?

Knock, knock.
Who's there?
Toucan.
Toucan who?
Toucan live as cheaply as one.

Knock, knock.
Who's there?
Mustang.
Mustang who?
I mustang this lovely picture on the wall.

Knock, knock.
Who's there?
Newt.
Newt who?
What's newt with you?

Knock, knock.
Who's there?
Wildebeest.
Wildebeest who?
Wildebeest turn back into a prince?

Knock, knock.
Who's there?
Paws.
Paws who?
Paws-itively delighted
to see you!

Knock, knock.
Who's there?
Phyllis.
Phyllis who?
Phyllis trough up with water, please. The cows are thirsty!

Knock, knock.
Who's there?
Pig.
Pig who?
Pig up your toys. Your room is a mess!

Knock, knock.
Who's there?
Tweet.
Tweet who?
Tweet me nicely, and I'll tweet you nicely, too.

Knock, knock.
Who's there?
Puffin.
Puffin who?
Puffin' and pantin' after running
all the way here.

Knock, knock.
Who's there?
Purring.
Purring who?
Purring some lemonade. Do you want some?

Knock, knock.
Who's there?
Rabbit.
Rabbit who?
Please rabbit up for me—I'll eat it for lunch.

Knock, knock.
Who's there?
Raven.
Raven who?
I've been raven about you to all my friends!

Knock, knock.
Who's there?
Sssssss.
Sssssss *who?*
Make up your mind. Are you a snake or an owl?

Knock, knock.
Who's there?
Swan.
Swan who?
Just swan to say *hi.*

Knock, knock.
Who's there?
Tail.
Tail who?
Tail me you love me!

Knock, knock.
Who's there?
Kelp.
Kelp who?
Kelp, a crab is pinching my toe!

Knock, knock.
Who's there?
Talon.
Talon who?
Talon everyone I know that you're the best.

Knock, knock.
Who's there?
Toad.
Toad who?
If I toad you, would you open the door?

Knock, knock.
Who's there?
Crows.
Crows who?
Crows the door. It's cold outside!

Knock, knock.
Who's there?
Turtle.
Turtle who?
Got to go. Turtle-oo.

Knock, knock.
Who's there?
Tusk.
Tusk who?
Tusk, tusk, it looks like rain.

Knock, knock.
Who's there?
Pigment.
Pigment who?
Pigment a lot to me, but he ran away.

Knock, knock.
Who's there?
Ladies.
Ladies who?
A chicken ladies eggs.

Knock, knock.
Who's there?
Whale.
Whale who?
Whale you be mine?

Knock, knock.
Who's there?
Ooze.
Ooze who?
Ooze a good dog?

Knock, knock.
Who's there?
Wing.
Wing who?
Wing, wing, wing. Hello?

Knock, knock.
Who's there?
Furry.
Furry who?
Furry funny jokes we're telling today.

Knock, knock.
Who's there?
Wren.
Wren who?
Wren are you going to let me in?

Knock, knock.
Who's there?
Interrupting sheep.
Interrup—
BAAAAA!

Knock, knock.
Who's there?
Yorkies.
Yorkies who?
Yorkies don't fit in the lock!

Knock, knock.
Who's there?
Toucan.
Toucan who?
Toucan play checkers, but only one can win.

Knock, knock.
Who's there?
Zoo.
Zoo who?
Zoo should come again!

Knock, knock.
Who's there?
Waddle.
Waddle who?
Waddle you give me if I tell you?

Knock, knock.
Who's there?
Heron.
Heron who?
Heron the floor of the salon needs to be swept up.

Knock, knock.
Who's there?
Meerkat.
Meerkat who?
Meerkat, 'meer kitty, come get your treat!

Knock, knock.
Who's there?
Mule.
Mule who?
Mule miss me, won't you?

Knock, knock.
Who's there?
A herd.
A herd who?
A herd you the first time.

Knock, knock.
Who's there?
Penguin.
Penguin who?
Penguin run out of ink after all that writing.

Knock, knock.
Who's there?
Frieda.
Frieda who?
Frieda horse, it's lunchtime.

Knock, knock.
Who's there?
Pig.
Pig who?
I'll need to pig the lock if you don't open up.

Knock, knock.
Who's there?
Oink.
Oink *who?*
Make up your mind. Are you a pig or an owl?

Knock, knock.
Who's there?
Duck.
Duck who?
Just duck! They're throwing snowballs at us!

Knock, knock.
Who's there?
Champ.
Champ who?
Champ-oo the dog. He needs a bath!

Knock, knock.
Who's there?
Hello.
Hello who?
Hello Kitty.

Knock, knock.
Who's there?
Kanga.
Kanga who?
Actually, it's kangaroo here for you!

Knock, knock.
Who's there?
Ewe.
Ewe who?
Ewe are my best friend.

Knock, knock.
Who's there?
An udder.
An udder who?
An udder-ly bad joke.

Knock, knock.
Who's there?
Bear.
Bear who?
Bear with me—we're not there yet.

Knock, knock.
Who's there?
Terrier.
Terrier who?
I'm terrier-fied of the dark!

Knock, knock.
Who's there?
Armadillo.
Armadillo who?
Armadillo the cards after you cut the deck.

Knock, knock.
Who's there?
Chesterfield.
Chesterfield who?
Chesterfield full of cows.

Knock, knock.
Who's there?
Ella.
Ella who?
Ella-phants are my favorite animal.

Knock, knock.
Who's there?
Neigh.
Neigh *who?*
Neigh-body listens to me!

Knock, knock.

Who's there?

Caden.

Caden who?

O-Caden, I won't tell you another knock-knock joke.

Knock, knock.
Who's there?
Arthur.
Arthur who?
Arthur-mometer is broken.

Knock, knock.
Who's there?
Max.
Max who?
It Max no difference—open the door.

Knock, knock.
Who's there?
Benjamin.
Benjamin who?
Benjamin to tunes all day!

Knock, knock.
Who's there?
Norton.
Norton who?
I've got Norton to say.

Knock, knock.
Who's there?
Doug.
Doug who?
Doug a hole looking for gold.

Knock, knock.
Who's there?
Ben.
Ben who?
Ben saving all my money for this new game!

Knock, knock.
Who's there?
Drew.
Drew who?
Drew you a picture. Want to see it?

Knock, knock.
Who's there?
Earl.
Earl who?
Early bird gets
the worm.

Knock, knock.
Who's there?
Eddie.
Eddie who?
Eddie-body got a tissue?
I have a terrible cold!

Knock, knock.
Who's there?
Harry.
Harry who?
Harry dogs go to the groomer.

Knock, knock.
Who's there?
Farley.
Farley who?
Farley the leader.

Knock, knock.
Who's there?
Gary.
Gary who?
Keep calm and Gary on!

Knock, knock.
Who's there?
Harris.
Harris who?
Harris knotted. Please help me comb it.

Knock, knock.
Who's there?
Logan.
Logan who?
Logan see who's at the door.

Knock, knock.
Who's there?
Elijah.
Elijah who?
Elijah down and won't get up.

Knock, knock.
Who's there?
Theodore.
Theodore who?
If you hadn't shut Theodore, I wouldn't be locked out.

Knock, knock.
Who's there?
Hutch.
Hutch who?
I'm sorry I made you sneeze!

Knock, knock.
Who's there?
Lee King.
Lee King who?
Lee King faucet won't stop dripping.

Knock, knock.
Who's there?
Agnew.
Agnew who?
Agnew you were going to post that.

Knock, knock.
Who's there?
Micah.
Micah who?
Micah is double-parked—hurry up!

Knock, knock.
Who's there?
Noah.
Noah who?
Noah-body!

Knock, knock.
Who's there?
Don.
Don who?
Don scream, but there's a spider by your foot.

Knock, knock.
Who's there?
Oliver.
Oliver who?
Oliver the world, people love candy.

Knock, knock.
Who's there?
Oscar and Greta.
Oscar and Greta who?
Oscar foolish question, Greta foolish answer.

Knock, knock.
Who's there?
Philip.
Philip who?
Philip my cup—I'm thirsty!

Knock, knock.
Who's there?
Rufus.
Rufus who?
Rufus leaking. You'd better get it fixed.

Knock, knock.
Who's there?
Sherwood.
Sherwood who?
Sherwood like you to open the door!

Knock, knock.
Who's there?
Stu.
Stu who?
Stu late to be answering the door.

Knock, knock.
Who's there?
Thaddeus.
Thaddeus who?
Thaddeus what I want to know!

Knock, knock.
Who's there?
Hurley.
Hurley who?
Hurley to bed, Hurley to rise.

Knock, knock.
Who's there?
Van.
Van who?
Van will YOU tell ME a joke?

Knock, knock.
Who's there?
Wade.
Wade who?
Wade a minute and I will tell you.

Knock, knock.
Who's there?
Ahab.
Ahab who?
Ahab to go to the bathroom. Open the door!

Knock, knock.
Who's there?
Wiley.
Wiley who?
Wiley was out, a package
was delivered.

Knock, knock.
Who's there?
Roland.
Roland who?
Roland butter sounds delicious.

Knock, knock.
Who's there?
Ben.
Ben who?
Ben away for a while, but now I'm back.

Knock, knock.
Who's there?
Raoul.
Raoul who?
Raoul with the punches.

Knock, knock.
Who's there?
Luke.
Luke who?
Luke-lele, play me a song.

Knock, knock.
Who's there?
Woody.
Woody who?
Woody like to come out and play?

Knock, knock.
Who's there?
Noah.
Noah who?
Noah good place to eat around here?

Knock, knock.
Who's there?
Billie Bob Ben Mackey.
Billie Bob Ben Mackey who?
Seriously, how many Billie Bob Ben Mackeys
do you know?

Knock, knock.
Who's there?
Howie.
Howie who?
Do you know Howie doing?

Knock, knock.
Who's there?
Gus.
Gus who?
Gus you don't want another slice of pizza.

Knock, knock.
Who's there?
Kyle.
Kyle who?
Kyle you were out, someone knocked.

Knock, knock.
Who's there?
Renato.
Renato who?
Renato gas for my car!

Knock, knock.
Who's there?
Nicholas.
Nicholas who?
A Nicholas not much money these days.

Knock, knock.
Who's there?
Brad.
Brad who?
Brad news, I'm afraid.

Knock, knock.
Who's there?
Uriah.
Uriah who?
Keep Uriah on the ball.

Knock, knock.
Who's there?
Watson.
Watson who?
Watson your mind?

Knock, knock.
Who's there?
Archibald.
Archibald who?
Archibald babies just the cutest?

Knock, knock.
Who's there?
Michael.
Michael who?
I Michael you on the phone if you don't let me in.

Knock, knock.
Who's there?
Buster.
Buster who?
Buster tire, can I use your phone?

Knock, knock.
Who's there?
Dwight.
Dwight who?
Dwight way is better than the wrong way.

Knock, knock.
Who's there?
Bernie.
Bernie who?
Bernie the cake and it tastes terrible.

Knock, knock.
Who's there?
Patrick.
Patrick who?
Patrick or treat and we'll get candy.

Knock, knock.
Who's there?
James.
James who?
James people play!

Knock, knock.
Who's there?
Kent.
Kent who?
I Kent see why you won't just open the door.

Knock, knock.
Who's there?
Orville.
Orville who?
Orville I see you tomorrow?

Knock, knock.
Who's there?
Stan.
Stan who?
I can't Stan another knock-knock joke.

Knock, knock.
Who's there?
Colin.
Colin who?
From now on I'm Colin you
on the phone.

Knock, knock.
Who's there?
Liam.
Liam who?
Liam alone. He's in a bad mood.

Knock, knock.
Who's there?
Bill.
Bill who?
I'll pay the Bill for dinner if you let me in.

Knock, knock.
Who's there?
Conner.
Conner who?
Conner tell me another joke as funny as the last one?

Knock, knock.
Who's there?
Thatcher.
Thatcher who?
Thatcher was a good joke.
Can you tell me another?

Knock, knock.
Who's there?
Asher.
Asher who?
Asher mom if we can have a snack.

Knock, knock.
Who's there?
Mason.
Mason who?
Mason-shine light your way.

Knock, knock.
Who's there?
Fred.
Fred who?
Fred I can't come out today!

Knock, knock.
Who's there?
Bert.
Bert who?
Bert the dinner. We'll have to go out.

Knock, knock.
Who's there?
Keith.
Keith who?
Keith calm, we'll find our way home.

Knock, knock.
Who's there?
Luke.
Luke who?
Lukewarm is how I like my tea.

Knock, knock.
Who's there?
Dewey.
Dewey who?
Dewey have to listen to all this knocking?

Knock, knock.

Who's there?

Tim.

Tim who?

Timber! Look out for that tree!

Knock, knock.

Who's there?

Ron.

Ron who?

Ron away, but I'll still catch you!

Knock, knock.
Who's there?
Joe.
Joe who?
Just Joe-king. Never mind.

Knock, knock.
Who's there?
Dwayne.
Dwayne who?
Dwayne the bathtub before it overflows!

Knock, knock.
Who's there?
Arnie.
Arnie who?
Arnie-ments are fun to put on the tree.

Camping Cackles

Knock, knock.
Who's there?
Arthur.
Arthur who?
Arthur any spiders in this tent?

Knock, knock.
Who's there?
S'more.
S'more who?
Camping is s'more fun
with friends.

Knock, knock.
Who's there?
Hike.
Hike who?
I didn't know you liked poetry.

Knock, knock.
Who's there?
Matt.
Matt who?
Mattresses here are hard as rocks.

Knock, knock.
Who's there?
Spider.
Spider who?
Spider the rain, we still had a fun camping trip.

Knock, knock.
Who's there?
Icing.
Icing who?
Icing camp songs around the fire.

Knock, knock.
Who's there?
Edward.
Edward who?
Edward be nice if you cleaned the cabin.

Knock, knock.
Who's there?
Accordion.
Accordion who?
Accordion to my compass, the campsite is over the hill.

Knock, knock.
Who's there?
Tents.
Tents who?
Tents? You should try to relax.

Knock, knock.

Who's there?

Marsha.

Marsha who?

Marsha-mellows are great for toasting.

Knock, knock.
Who's there?
Owl.
Owl who?
Owl help you pitch your tent.

Knock, knock.
Who's there?
Scott.
Scott who?
Scott to be a bear around here somewhere.

Knock, knock.
Who's there?
Moose.
Moose who?
Moose-quitos kept biting me on the hike.

Knock, knock.
Who's there?
Tree.
Tree who?
It's tree-mendous to camp with you.

Knock, knock.
Who's there?
Alec.
Alec who?
Alec camping, but not when it rains.

Knock, knock.
Who's there?
Alison.
Alison who?
Alison it's dark outside!
Where's the lantern?

Knock, knock.
Who's there?
Alda.
Alda who?
Alda campers love s'mores.

Knock, knock.
Who's there?
Ken.
Ken who?
Ken you hear something growling?

Knock, knock.
Who's there?
Canoe.
Canoe who?
Canoe help me put up the tent?

Knock, knock.
Who's there?
Kerry.
Kerry who?
Kerry on with the hike—
it's just a little further!

Knock, knock.
Who's there?
Howdy.
Howdy who?
Howdy spider get in my tent?

Knock, knock.
Who's there?
Leaf.
Leaf who?
Leaf me alone. I'm trying to sleep.

Knock, knock.
Who's there?
Fire.
Fire who?
Fire you standing there? Get an extinguisher.

Knock, knock.
Who's there?
Water.
Water who?
Water you doing in the lake?

Knock, knock.
Who's there?
Kayak.
Kayak who?
Quit your kayak-ing and start paddling.

Knock, knock.
Who's there?
RV.
RV who?
RV there yet?

Knock, knock.
Who's there?
Summertime.
Summertime who?
Summertime I'll open up, but not now.

Knock, knock.
Who's there?
Claws.
Claws who?
Claws the tent flap—it's raining.

Knock, knock.
Who's there?
Alex.
Alex who?
Alex the counselor if we can go swimming.

Knock, knock.
Who's there?
Dawn.
Dawn who?
Dawn wake me up so early.

Knock, knock.
Who's there?
Knot.
Knot who?
Knot another knock-knock joke, please!

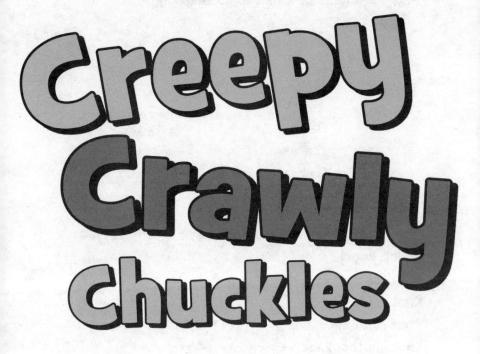

Creepy Crawly Chuckles

Knock, knock.
Who's there?
Henrietta.
Henrietta who?
Henrietta worm that was in his apple.

Knock, knock.
Who's there?
Anthill.
Anthill who?
Anthill we meet again.

Knock, knock.
Who's there?
Bee.
Bee who?
Bee-cause I like you, I came to visit.

Knock, knock.
Who's there?
Patty.
Patty who?
Patty longlegs are big arachnids.

Knock, knock.
Who's there?
Beetle.
Beetle who?
Beetle little more flour into the dough, will you?

Knock, knock.
Who's there?
Ant.
Ant who?
Ant this music great?

Knock, knock.
Who's there?
Fleas.
Fleas who?
"Fleas a jolly good fellow . . ."

Knock, knock.
Who's there?
Mantis.
Mantis who?
Mantis music is groovy!

Knock, knock.
Who's there?
Pillar.
Pillar who?
A caterpillar has 16 legs!

Knock, knock.
Who's there?
Tick.
Tick who?
Ticktock, time is flying!

Knock, knock.
Who's there?
Moth.
Moth who?
I moth tell you that I like you!

Knock, knock.
Who's there?
Roach.
Roach who?
Roach you a letter—it's in the mail!

Knock, knock.
Who's there?
Termites.
Termites who?
Termite's the night the circus opens.

Knock, knock.
Who's there?
Free.
Free who?
A free is biting
my dog.

Knock, knock.
Who's there?
Worm.
Worm who?
Worm my keys go?

Knock, knock.
Who's there?
Stew.
Stew who?
Stew many moths. Turn out the light.

Knock, knock.
Who's there?
Yeti.
Yeti who?
Yeti-nother mosquito.

Knock, knock.
Who's there?
Beezer.
Beezer who?
Beezer buzzing.
It must be spring.

Knock, knock.
Who's there?
Amos.
Amos who?
Amos-quito just bit me!

Knock, knock.
Who's there?
Thumping.
Thumping who?
Watch out! Thumping creepy is crawling up behind you!

Knock, knock.
Who's there?
Spider.
Spider who?
I spider-licious dinner headed my way.

Knock, knock.
Who's there?
Flea.
Flea who?
One, two, flea . . . go!

Knock, knock.
Who's there?
Larva.
Larva who?
I larva you!

Knock, knock.
Who's there?
Wasp.
Wasp who?
I wasp planning to tell you.

Knock, knock.
Who's there?
Beehive.
Beehive who?
Bee-hive yourself or we'll have to go.

Knock, knock.

Who's there?

Lady.

Lady who?

Ladybugs are married to lordbugs.

Knock, knock.

Who's there?

Roach.

Roach who?

Roach out and touch someone!

Knock, knock.

Who's there?

Army ants.

Army ants who?

Army ants coming for tea?

Knock, knock.
Who's there?
Glass.
Glass who?
Glass-hoppers have two pairs of wings.

Knock, knock.
Who's there?
ABCs.
ABCs who?
ABCs a flower and lands on it.

Knock, knock.
Who's there?
Butterflies.
Butterflies who?
Butterflies off the shelves when
it's on sale at the grocery store.

Dinosaur Crack-Ups

Knock, knock.
Who's there?
Norah.
Norah who?
Norah good joke about dinosaurs?

Knock, knock.
Who's there?
Dinosaurs.
Dinosaurs who?
Dinosaurs through the air in a plane.

Knock, knock.
Who's there?
Steak.
Steak who?
Steak-osaurus was
a plant eater.

Knock, knock.
Who's there?
Adam.
Adam who?
Adam my way, please. There's a *T. rex* chasing me!

Knock, knock.
Who's there?
Shale.
Shale who?
Shale we go see the new fossil exhibit?

Knock, knock.
Who's there?
Dewey.
Dewey who?
Dewey know why the dinosaurs went extinct?

Knock, knock.
Who's there?
Dinosaur go.
Dinosaur go who?
Dinosaurs don't go *who*. They go *ROAR!*

Knock, knock.
Who's there?
Detail.
Detail who?
Detail of de dino
is on de end.

DE
DINO

DE
TAIL

DE
END

Knock, knock.
Who's there?
Stan.
Stan who?
Stan back when a dinosaur sneezes!

Knock, knock.
Who's there?
Meteor.
Meteor who?
Meteor snacks are a carnivore's favorite.

Knock, knock.
Who's there?
Tyrannosaurus rex.
Tyrannosaurus rex *who?*
Tyrannosaurus rex his car and can't get to work.

Knock, knock.
Who's there?
Floss.
Floss who?
Floss-iraptors have the best
dental hygiene.

Knock, knock.
Who's there?
Four eggs.
Four eggs who?
Four eggs-ample, there
are only three types
of dinosaur eggs.

Knock, knock.
Who's there?
Annie.
Annie who?
Annie-one see the new dinosaur
exhibit at the museum?

Knock, knock.
Who's there?
Tara.
Tara who?
Tara-dactyls weren't dinosaurs.
They were flying reptiles!

Knock, knock.
Who's there?
Wendy.
Wendy who?
Wendy dinosaurs went extinct,
de Mesozoic Era ended.

Knock, knock.
Who's there?
Kenya.
Kenya who?
Kenya guess which fossils were found in Africa?

Knock, knock.
Who's there?
Raptor.
Raptor who?
Raptor not, your friend will
still love the birthday gift.

HA

103

Knock, knock.
Who's there?
Dinosaur.
Dinosaur who?
Dinosaur and needs an ice pack.

Knock, knock.
Who's there?
Ice cream.
Ice cream who?
Ice cream when I see a dinosaur—don't you?

Knock, knock.
Who's there?
Ada.
Ada who?
"Ada whole tree for lunch," said the *Stegosaurus.*

Knock, knock.
Who's there?
Chicken.
Chicken who?
Chicken the encyclopedia—
birds are related to dinosaurs.

Knock, knock.
Who's there?
Dynamite.
Dynamite who?
Dynamite have left a fossilized footprint.

Knock, knock.
Who's there?
Extinct.
Extinct who?
Extinct when they go bad.

Knock, knock.
Who's there?
Ankle.
Ankle who?
Ankle-osaurus was an armored dinosaur.

Knock, knock.
Who's there?
Terror.
Terror who?
Terror-dactyls were one of the
scariest prehistoric animals.

Knock, knock.

Who's there?

Shirley.

Shirley who?

Shirley this is the last dinosaur joke.

Knock, knock.
Who's there?
Ammonia.
Ammonia who?
Ammonia little kid!

Knock, knock.
Who's there.
Farther.
Farther who?
Like farther, like son.

Knock, knock.
Who's there?
Justin.
Justin who?
Justin time for dinner!

Knock, knock.
Who's there?
Orchid.
Orchid who?
Orchid is so funny. I bet every parent thinks so!

Knock, knock.
Who's there?
Whale.
Whale who?
Whale-come home from work!

Knock, knock.
Who's there?
Son.
Son who?
Son-day is the best day of the week.

Knock, knock.
Who's there?
Lena.
Lena who?
Lena little closer and give me a kiss.

Knock, knock.
Who's there?
Little girl.
Little girl who?
Little girl who can't reach the doorbell!

Knock, knock.
Who's there?
Paws.
Paws who?
Paws the movie, Mom, please. I'm getting a snack!

Knock, knock.
Who's there?
Philippa.
Philippa who?
Philippa plate and sit down for dinner.

Knock, knock.
Who's there?
Pear.
Pear who?
Pear-ents just don't understand.

Knock, knock.
Who's there?
Pizza.
Pizza who?
Pass a pizza the cake.

Knock, knock.
Who's there?
Rita.
Rita who?
Rita book. They're better
than movies.

Knock, knock.
Who's there?
Summertime.
Summertime who?
Summertime the cat lets you pet him,
and summertime he doesn't.

Knock, knock.
Who's there?
Uno.
Uno who?
Uno where your brother is?

Knock, knock.
Who's there?
Irma.
Irma who?
Irma big girl now.

Knock, knock.

Who's there?

Canoe.

Canoe who?

Canoe babysit Saturday night?

Knock, knock.

Who's there?

Yoda.

Yoda who?

Yoda best, Grandpa!

Knock, knock.
Who's there?
Granny.
Granny who?
Knock, knock.
Who's there?
Granny.
Granny who?
Knock, knock.
Who's there?
Aunt.
Aunt who?
Aunt you glad Granny's gone home?

      Knock, knock.
      Who's there?
      Mary.
      Mary who?
      Mary me and I'll love you forever!

Knock, knock.
Who's there?
Nerf.
Nerf who?
Your nerf-ew is here for a visit.

Knock, knock.
Who's there?
Bud.
Bud who?
Bud is thicker than water.

Knock, knock.
Who's there?
Little old lady.
Little old lady who?
I didn't know you could yodel.

Knock, knock.
Who's there?
Batter.
Batter who?
What's a batter, baby? Why are you crying?

Knock, knock.
Who's there?
Yacht.
Yacht who?
Yacht to be able to recognize your
own brother, surely!

Knock, knock.

Who's there?

Acute.

Acute who?

Acute little sister wants to dance!

Knock, knock.
Who's there?
Kate.
Kate who?
Which twin sister is the dupli-Kate?

Knock, knock.
Who's there?
Hayden.
Hayden who?
Come out and let's play Hayden-go-seek.

Knock, knock.
Who's there?
Instagram.
Instagram who?
Instagram-a at the door. Let her in!

Knock, knock.
Who's there?
Pickle.
Pickle who?
Pickle little flower for your mother.

Knock, knock.

Who's there?

Bison.

Bison who?

Bison, have a good day at school.

Knock, knock.
Who's there?
Eeyore.
Eeyore who?
Eeyore is locked. Let me in.

Knock, knock.
Who's there?
Grateful.
Grateful who?
Humpty Dumpty had a grateful.

Knock, knock.

Who's there?

Barbie.

Barbie who?

Time to Barbie-cue!

Knock, knock.

Who's there?

Surrender.

Surrender who?

Surrender is a knight afraid to fight.

Knock, knock.
Who's there?
Quidditch.
Quidditch who?
Quidditch-ing that bugbite. You are making it worse.

Knock, knock.
Who's there?
Soup.
Soup who?

Soup-erman is able to leap tall buildings with a single bound.

Knock, knock.
Who's there?
Tom Hanks.
Tom Hanks who?
Tom, Hanks for being such a good friend.

Knock, knock.
Who's there?
Hog.
Hog who?
Hogwarts School of Witchcraft and Wizardry.

Knock, knock.

Who's there?

Merry.

Merry who?

Merry Poppins is a magical nanny.

Knock, knock.

Who's there?

Water.

Water who?

Water you doing living in a pineapple, Spongebob?

Knock, knock.

Who's there?

Watermelon.

Watermelon who?

Watermelon DeGeneres is the voice of Dory.

Knock, knock.
Who's there?
Nana.
Nana who?
"Nana nana nana nana Batman!"

Knock, knock.
Who's there?
Snow.
Snow who?
"Snow business like snow business like snow business I know."

Knock, knock.
Who's there?
Oscar.
Oscar who?
Oscar if she wants to go to an awards show.

Knock, knock.
Who's there?
Mickey.
Mickey who?
Mickey broke, so I can't lock the door.

Knock, knock.
Who's there?
Hobbits.
Hobbits who?
Hobbits going out for ice cream later?

Knock, knock.
Who's there?
Doctor.
Doctor who?
That's my favorite science
fiction show!

Knock, knock.
Who's there?
Wand.
Wand who?
The wand-erful Wizard of Oz.

Knock, knock.
Who's there?
Thor.
Thor who?
Thor-ry, I think I have the wrong house.

Knock, knock.

Who's there?

Tinkerbell.

Tinkerbell who?

Tinkerbell is not working. That is why I am knocking.

Knock, knock.

Who's there?

Web.

Web who?

Web-ruary is Spiderman's favorite month.

Knock, knock.
Who's there?
Cam.
Cam who?
Camelot is where King Arthur lived!

Knock, knock.
Who's there?
Bus.
Bus who?
Bus Lightyear to the rescue!

Knock, knock.
Who's there?
Actor.
Actor who?
Actor you, my dear sir.

Knock, knock.
Who's there?
Yukon.
Yukon who?
Yukon see a lot of stars on the Hollywood Walk of Fame.

Knock, knock.
Who's there?
Godfrey.
Godfrey who?
Godfrey tickets to Cinderella's ball.
Want to come?

Knock, knock.
Who's there?
Winnie-thup.
Winnie-thup who?
You've got it! Winnie-the-Pooh!

Knock, knock.
Who's there?
Deduct.
Deduct who?
Donald Deduct.

Knock, knock.
Who's there?
Robin.
Robin who?
Robin Hood's known for robin' the rich.

Knock, knock.
Who's there?
Elly.
Elly who?
Elly-mentary, my dear Watson!

Knock, knock.
Who's there?
Holly.
Holly who?
Hollywood is calling—time to star in a movie!

Knock, knock.
Who's there?
Nemo.
Nemo who?
Nemo jokes? I know hundreds!

Knock, knock.
Who's there?
Snow.
Snow who?
"Snow place like home," said Dorothy.

Knock, knock.
Who's there?
May the fourth.
May the fourth who?
May the fourth be with you!

Knock, knock.
Who's there?
Scavengers.
Scavengers who?
Scavengers Assemble!

Knock, knock.

Who's there?

Warts.

Warts who?

Star Warts is my frog's favorite movie.

Knock, knock.
Who's there?
Art.
Art who?
Art2-D2!

Knock, knock.
Who's there?
Boba Fett.
Boba Fett who?
Boba Fett my goldfish.

Knock, knock.
Who's there.
Ewok.
Ewok who?
Ewok-ed the door. Let me in!

Knock, knock.
Who's there?
Yoda.
Yoda who?
Yoda one who wanted to hear a knock-knock joke.

Funny Food

Knock, knock.

Who's there?

Peas.

Peas who?

Peas to meet you.

Knock, knock.
Who's there?
Sushi.
Sushi who?
She believed she could, sushi did.

Knock, knock.
Who's there?
Anita.
Anita who?
Anita snack. Let's eat!

Knock, knock.
Who's there?
Barley.
Barley who?
I can barley wait!

Knock, knock.
Who's there?
Atomic.
Atomic who?
I have atomic-ache from
eating all this candy.

Knock, knock.
Who's there?
Butcher.
Butcher who?
"You butcher left leg in,
you butcher left leg out . . ."

Knock, knock.
Who's there?
Butter.
Butter who?
Butter get ready
for the party.
It starts in 10 minutes!

Knock, knock.
Who's there?
Abraham.
Abraham who?
Abraham and cheese sandwich, please!

Knock, knock.
Who's there?
Pudding.
Pudding who?
Pudding whipped cream on pie is delicious.

Knock, knock.
Who's there?
Salami.
Salami who?
Salami get this straight.

Knock, knock.
Who's there?
Kale.
Kale who?
Here's my number. Kale me!

Knock, knock.
Who's there?
Gouda.
Gouda who?
She's a Gouda friend.

Knock, knock.

Who's there?

Cantaloupe.

Cantaloupe who?

We cantaloupe tonight—I forgot the rings.

Knock, knock.

Who's there?

Catapult.

Catapult who.

Catapult the tablecloth down and our dinner went flying!

Knock, knock.
Who's there?
Bean.
Bean who?
Bean there, done that.

Knock, knock.
Who's there?
Bacon.
Bacon who?
I'm bacon a cake for
your birthday!

Knock, knock.
Who's there?
Egg.
Egg who?
I'm egg-cited to meet you!

Knock, knock.
Who's there?
Falafel.
Falafel who?
I falafel my bike and hurt my knee.

Knock, knock.
Who's there?
Beet.
Beet who?
The beet goes on.

Knock, knock.
Who's there?
Handsome.
Handsome who?
Handsome of those
cookies over, please.

Knock, knock.
Who's there?
Hammond.
Hammond who?
Hammond eggs is a great breakfast.

Knock, knock.
Who's there?
Howdy.
Howdy who?
Howdy-licious are those noodles?

Knock, knock.
Who's there?
Sammy Chez.
Sammy Chez who?
Sammy Chez are my favorite food to eat for lunch.

Knock, knock.
Who's there?
Hummus.
Hummus who?
Hummus be kidding!

Knock, knock.
Who's there?
Raisin.
Raisin who?
No raisin to be so sad.

Knock, knock.
Who's there?
Grape.
Grape who?
Grape to see you again!

Knock, knock.
Who's there?
Kiwi.
Kiwi who?
Kiwi come inside?

Knock, knock.
Who's there?
Lemon.
Lemon who?
Lemon introduce myself.

Knock, knock.
Who's there?
Ice-cream soda.
Ice-cream soda who?
Ice-cream soda whole
neighborhood can hear me.

Knock, knock.
Who's there?
Lime.
Lime who?
Lime leaving if you don't
open the door!

Knock, knock.
Who's there?
Mint.
Mint who?
I mint to tell you sooner
that I was coming over.

Knock, knock.
Who's there?
Tomatoes.
Tomatoes who?
From ma head tomatoes.

Knock, knock.
Who's there?
Paris.
Paris who?
A Paris good, but I'd rather have an orange.

Knock, knock.
Who's there?
Pickle.
Pickle who?
Pickle on someone your own size!

Knock, knock.
Who's there?
Rice.
Rice who?
Rice up early every morning.

Knock, knock.
Who's there?
Ricotta.
Ricotta who?
Ricotta new puppy. Want to pet it?

Knock, knock.
Who's there?
Potato.
Potato who?
Potatoes don't have
last names, silly!

Knock, knock.

Who's there?
Ketchup.
Ketchup who?
Ketchup, or
you'll be late!

Knock, knock.
Who's there?
Soda.
Soda who?
Soda reason I'm knocking is to say *hello*!

Knock, knock.
Who's there?
Berry.
Berry who?
Berry nice to meet you!

149

Knock, knock.
Who's there?
Stirrup.
Stirrup who?
Stirrup some hot chocolate
for me, please.

Knock, knock.
Who's there?
Turnip.
Turnip who?
Turnip the light! I'm scared.

Knock, knock.
Who's there?
Ramon.
Ramon who?
Ramon noodle soup is delicious!

Knock, knock.
Who's there?
Figs.
Figs who?
Figs the doorbell so I don't have to knock.

Knock, knock.
Who's there?
Cheese.
Cheese who?
Cheese a good waitress.

Knock, knock.
Who's there?
Orange.
Orange who?
Orange you going to read the rest
of these knock-knock jokes?

Knock, knock.
Who's there?
Taco.
Taco who?
I don't want to taco-bout it.

Knock, knock.

Who's there?

Waffle.

Waffle who?

Waffle lot of fireflies out tonight.

Knock, knock.
Who's there?
Selfish.
Selfish who?
I'm allergic to selfish, so no oysters for me.

Knock, knock.
Who's there?
Tom.
Tom who?
No Tomato on my sandwich, please.

Knock, knock.
Who's there?
Curry.
Curry who?
Curry me back home, will you?

Knock, knock.
Who's there?
Fry.
Fry who?
Fry-day we'll go out to dinner.

Knock, knock.
Who's there?
Sue.
Sue who?
Grew some Sue-cchini in my garden. Want some?

Knock, knock.
Who's there?
Inch.
Inch who?
Inch-iladas are my favorite Mexican food.

Knock, knock.
Who's there?
Vendors.
Vendors who?
Chicken vendors are good with honey mustard.

Knock, knock.
Who's there?
Pizza.
Pizza who?
I'm going to give him a pizza my mind!

Knock, knock.
Who's there?
Cannelloni.
Cannelloni who?
Cannelloni some money till next week?

Knock, knock.
Who's there?
Beef.
Beef who?
Beef-ore I get cold, you'd better let me in!

Knock, knock.
Who's there?
Lynn.
Lynn who?
Want Lynn-guini with tomato sauce for dinner?

ha
ha

Knock, knock.
Who's there?
Doughnut.
Doughnut who?
Doughnut make you laugh when
you hear a knock-knock joke?

Knock, knock.
Who's there?
Muffin.
Muffin who?
Muffin much going on around here.

Knock, knock.
Who's there?
Steak.
Steak who?
Mi-steaks were made that need to be corrected.

Knock, knock.
Who's there?
Two knee.
Two knee who?
Two-knee fish!

Knock, knock.
Who's there?
Kara.
Kara who?
Kara-mel is best with chocolate.

Knock, knock.
Who's there?
Waiter.
Waiter who?
Waiter minute while I finish my tacos!

Knock, knock.
Who's there?
Eggs.
Eggs who?
Eggs-tremely disappointed you still don't recognize me.

Knock, knock.
Who's there?
Abby.
Abby who?
Abby good if you give me some candy.

Knock, knock.
Who's there?
Zoo.
Zoo who?
Zoo-cchini make great pasta.

Knock, knock.
Who's there?
Lentil.
Lentil who?
It's not over lentil it's over.

Knock, knock.

Who's there?

Loaf.

Loaf who?

I don't just like bread. I loaf it!

Knock, knock.

Who's there?

Icing.

Icing who?

Icing so loud, the neighbors can hear me.

Knock, knock.

Who's there?

Lettuce.

Lettuce who?

Lettuce see what jokes are on the next page.

Knock, knock.

Who's there?

Ammonia.

Ammonia who?

Ammonia beginner, but I love geography already.

Knock, knock.
Who's there?
Alaska.
Alaska who?
Alaska-nother joke about Alaska.

Knock, knock.
Who's there?
Juneau.
Juneau who?
Juneau where Alaska is?

Knock, knock.
Who's there?
Annapolis.
Annapolis who?
Annapolis a day makes you
want to play.

Knock, knock.
Who's there?
Texas.
Texas who?
Texas are getting higher every year!

Knock, knock.
Who's there?
Utah.
Utah who?
Utah a puddy tat?

Knock, knock.
Who's there?
Tennessee.
Tennessee who?
Tennessee you later at the movies?

Knock, knock.
Who's there?
Minnesota.
Minnesota who?
Minnesota is all I can drink.

Knock, knock.
Who's there?
Nevada.
Nevada who?
Bet you Nevada friend like me.

Knock, knock.
Who's there?
Harrisburg.
Harrisburg who?
Harrisburg-er for you.

Knock, knock.
Who's there?
Albany.
Albany who?
Albany-ing help with my homework!

Knock, knock.
Who's there?
Florida.
Florida who?
The Florida bathroom is wet.

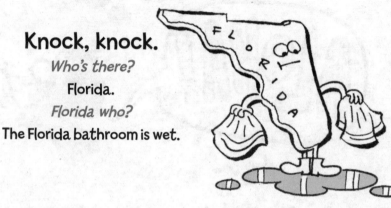

Knock, knock.
Who's there?
Kissimmee.
Kissimmee who?
Kissimmee a frog, and he'll turn into a prince!

Knock, knock.
Who's there?
Georgia.
Georgia who?
"Georgia the Jungle, watch out
for that tree."

Knock, knock.
Who's there?
Hawaii.
Hawaii who?
Hawaii doing today?

Knock, knock.
Who's there?
Al.
Al who?
Al be seeing you in Detroit.

Knock, knock.
Who's there?
Kansas.
Kansas who?
Kansas be the way to get home?

Knock, knock.
Who's there?
Hampshire.
Hampshire who?
Hampshire you aren't going to open the door.

Knock, knock.
Who's there?
Yukon.
Yukon who?
Yukon never get tired of geography jokes.

Knock, knock.
Who's there?
Utica.
Utica who?
Utica the high road.

Knock, knock.
Who's there?
Iowa.
Iowa who?
Iowa you a dollar!

Knock, knock.
Who's there?
Dublin.
Dublin who?
Dublin up with laughter at this great joke.

Knock, knock.
Who's there?
Egypt.
Egypt who?
Egypt you when he sold you
a broken doorbell.

Knock, knock.
Who's there?
Genoa.
Genoa who?
Genoa how to milk a cow?

Knock, knock.
Who's there?
Ma's cow.
Ma's cow who?
Ma's cow's the
capital of Russia.

Knock, knock.
Who's there?
Rio.
Rio who?
Want to hear a Rio funny joke?

Knock, knock.
Who's there?
Tibet.
Tibet who?
Make sure you get Tibet early.
You have school tomorrow!

Knock, knock.
Who's there?
Tijuana.
Tijuana who?
Tijuana hear another knock-knock joke?

Knock, knock.
Who's there?
Uruguay.
Uruguay who?
It's always Uruguay or the highway.

Knock, knock.
Who's there?
Pencil
Pencil who?
Pencil-vania is bordered by
six other states.

Knock, knock.
Who's there?
Lass.
Lass who?
Lass time I went to
Paris, I got lost!

Knock, knock.
Who's there?
Nile.
Nile who?
Nile down and tie your shoe. You don't want to trip!

Knock, knock.
Who's there?
Aunt.
Aunt who?
Aunt-arctica is the coldest continent!

Knock, knock.
Who's there?
Vera.
Vera who?
The Indian Ocean is Vera deep.

Knock, knock.
Who's there?
West.
West who?
Take a west from all
of these knock-knock jokes.

Knock, knock.
Who's there?
Tokyo.
Tokyo who?
What Tokyo so long to open the door?

Knock, knock.
Who's there?
India.
India who?
India good old summertime.

Knock, knock.
Who's there?
Ice pick.
Ice pick who?
Ice pick English but can understand some Spanish.

Knock, knock.
Who's there?
Israel.
Israel who?
Israel nice to meet you!

Knock, knock.

Who's there?

Whitney.

Whitney who?

Whitney river bends,
we call it a *meander.*

Knock, knock.

Who's there?

Quebec.

Quebec who?

Quebec to the end of the line!

Knock, knock.
Who's there?
Italy.
Italy who?
Italy a big job!

Knock, knock.
Who's there?
Canada.
Canada who?
Canada come and play, please?

Knock, knock.
Who's there?
China.
China who?
China just like old times, isn't it?

Knock, knock.
Who's there?
Guinea.
Guinea who?
Guinea a break!

Knock, knock.
Who's there?
Ireland.
Ireland who?
Ireland you money, if you promise to pay me back.

Knock, knock.
Who's there?
Russian.
Russian who?
Russian through your meal will make you sick!

Knock, knock.
Who's there?
Oman.
Oman who?
Oman, these jokes are bad!

Knock, knock.
Who's there?
Sweden.
Sweden who?
Sweden sour chicken is my favorite!

Knock, knock.
Who's there?
Uganda.
Uganda who?
Uganda get away with this!

Knock, knock.
Who's there?
Bolivia.
Bolivia who?
Don't Bolivia I've had the pleasure.

Knock, knock.
Who's there?
Chile.
Chile who?
It's getting Chile out here. Please let me in.

Knock, knock.
Who's there?
Congo.
Congo who?
You Congo home again.

Knock, knock.
Who's there?
Glasgow.
Glasgow who?
Glasgow to the beach.

Knock, knock.
Who's there?
Iraq.
Iraq who?
Iraq out to some good tunes.

Knock, knock.
Who's there?
Perth.
Perth who?
Hand me my Perth. I think
I have some money inside.

Knock, knock.
Who's there?
Laos.
Laos who?
I am at a Laos for words.

Knock, knock.
Who's there?
Berlin.
Berlin who?
I'm Berlin the water for hard-boiled eggs.

Knock, knock.
Who's there?
Rome.
Rome who?
Rome is where the heart is!

Knock, knock.
Who's there?
Red Sea.
Red Sea who?
Open the door, Red Sea for yourself.

Knock, knock.
Who's there?
Swiss.
Swiss who?
Swiss-consin is known for its cheese.

Knock, knock.
Who's there?
Spain.
Spain who?
So Spain why I should hire you.

Knock, knock.
Who's there?
Irish.
Irish who?
Irish you would let me in.

Knock, knock.
Who's there?
Suriname.
Suriname who?
Suriname Ariel? Because I think
we mermaid for each other.

Knock, knock.
Who's there?
Tehran.
Tehran who?
Tehran up the road in my car!

Knock, knock.
Who's there?
Tunis.
Tunis who?
Tunis company, three's a crowd!

Knock, knock.
Who's there?
Venice.
Venice who?
Venice your mom getting home?

Knock, knock.
Who's there?
Yemen.
Yemen who?
What do Yemen? I don't understand.

Knock, knock.
Who's there?
Toronto.
Toronto who?
Toronto be a law against so many knock-knock jokes.

Knock, knock.
Who's there?
France.
France who?
France are almost as close as family.

Knock, knock.
Who's there?
Lake.
Lake who?
I lake you a lot!

Knock, knock.
Who's there?
Denial.
Denial who?
Denial is a river in Egypt.

Knock, knock.
Who's there?
Norway.
Norway who?
There is Norway I'm going to just stand here, so open the door!

Knock, knock.
Who's there?
Tank.
Tank who?
Tank you for teaching me geography.

Knock, knock.
Who's there?
Kenya.
Kenya who?
Kenya fix the doorbell?
I've been knocking for hours!

Girl Name Giggles

Knock, knock.

Who's there?

Wanda.

Wanda who?

Wanda push me on the swings?

Knock, knock.

Who's there?

Della.

Della who?

Open the door so I can Della-nother knock-knock joke.

Knock, knock.

Who's there?

Julia.

Julia who?

Julia even know how to dance?

Knock, knock.
Who's there?
Blair.
Blair who?
Blair are you going?

Knock, knock.
Who's there?
Abby.
Abby who?
Abby stung me on my nose.

Knock, knock.
Who's there?
Odette.
Odette who?
Odette's a big improvement!

Knock, knock.
Who's there?
Theresa.
Theresa who?
Theresa storm coming. Let me in!

Knock, knock.
Who's there?
Annie.
Annie who?
Annie-one know where my dog is?

Knock, knock.
Who's there?
Doris.
Doris who?
Doris locked. Open up, please!

Knock, knock.
Who's there?
Megan.
Megan who?
Megan end to this joke, please!

Knock, knock.
Who's there?
Carrie.
Carrie who?
Carrie my books for me?

Knock, knock.
Who's there?
Maya.
Maya who?
Maya best friend?

Knock, knock.
Who's there?
Eliza.
Eliza who?
Eliza wake at night, counting sheep.

Knock, knock.
Who's there?
Sacha.
Sacha who?
You make Sacha fuss!

Knock, knock.
Who's there?
Gwen.
Gwen who?
Gwen-ever you wish.

Knock, knock.
Who's there?
Mindy.
Mindy who?
Mindy car. Can I call you back?

Knock, knock.
Who's there?
Fannie.
Fannie who?
Fannie-body asks, I've
gone bird-watching.

Knock, knock.

Who's there?

Heidi.

Heidi who?

Heidi bone in the yard.

Knock, knock.

Who's there?

Cass.

Cass who?

Cass more flies with honey than vinegar.

Knock, knock.
Who's there?
Leslie.
Leslie who?
Leslie down on the hammock.

Knock, knock.
Who's there?
Mia.
Mia who?
Mia-nd my shadow.

Knock, knock.
Who's there?
Eileen.
Eileen who?
Eileen over to pet the dog.

Knock, knock.
Who's there?
Isadora.
Isadora who?
Isadora locked, or can I come in?

Knock, knock.
Who's there?
Allison.
Allison who?
Allison to the birds sing every morning.

Knock, knock.
Who's there?
Olive.
Olive who?
And they Olive happily ever after.

Knock, knock.

Who's there?

Rhoda.

Rhoda who?

Rhoda camel through the desert.

Knock, knock.

Who's there?

Sabina.

Sabina who?

Sabina long time since I've heard a good joke!

Knock, knock.

Who's there?

Esther.

Esther who?

Esther any more cranberry sauce?

Knock, knock.
Who's there?
Molly.
Molly who?
Molly-cules make up everything!

Knock, knock.
Who's there?
Sadie.
Sadie who?
Sadie magic words, and I'll tell you.

Knock, knock.
Who's there?
Ava.
Ava who?
Ava seen the superhero movie?

Knock, knock.
Who's there?
Sarah.
Sarah who?
Sarah phone I could use?

Knock, knock.
Who's there?
Savannah.
Savannah who?
She's Savannah great time!

Knock, knock.
Who's there?
Anne.
Anne who?
I'll Anne-swer
your question
in a minute.

Knock, knock.
Who's there?
Sharon.
Sharon who?
You Sharon that pizza with me, or what?

Knock, knock.
Who's there?
Shirley.
Shirley who?
Shirley you know me. Let me in!

Knock, knock.
Who's there?
Winnie.
Winnie who?
Winnie gets home, you can ask your dad.

Knock, knock.
Who's there?
Tamara.
Tamara who?
Tamara is Tuesday.

Knock, knock.
Who's there?
Bea.
Bea who?
Bea-tween you and me, we have a problem.

Knock, knock.
Who's there?
Taylor.
Taylor who?
Taylor teacher she won't be in today.

Knock, knock.
Who's there?
Jan.
Jan who?
Jan-swer the door when someone knocks!

Knock, knock.
Who's there?
Charlotte.
Charlotte who?
Charlotte of knock-knock jokes!

Knock, knock.
Who's there?
Sloane.
Sloane who?
Sloane-ly, I could really use some company!

Knock, knock.

Who's there?

Wendy.

Wendy who?

Wendy bell works again, I won't have to knock anymore.

Knock, knock.
Who's there?
Emma.
Emma who?
Use your Emma-gination!

Knock, knock.
Who's there?
Susan.
Susan who?
Susan socks go on your feet.

Knock, knock.
Who's there?
Dawn.
Dawn who?
Dawn leave me out here in the cold!

Knock, knock.
Who's there?
Dee Wilson.
Dee Wilson who?
"Dee Wilson the bus go 'round and 'round."

Knock, knock.
Who's there?
Ivana.
Ivana who?
Ivana be rich!

Knock, knock.
Who's there?
Phoebe.
Phoebe who?
Entrance Phoebe too expensive for me!

Knock, knock.
Who's there?
Yolanda.
Yolanda who?
Yolanda me a dollar, I'll pay you back next week!

Knock, knock.

Who's there?

Amelia.

Amelia who?

Amelia a birthday card.

Knock, knock.

Who's there?

Aileen.

Aileen who?

Aileen against the wall because I'm cool.

Knock, knock.

Who's there?

Zoe.

Zoe who?

Zoe sidewalks are slippery.

Knock, knock.
Who's there?
Candice.
Candice who?
Candice get any better?

Knock, knock.
Who's there?
Sophia.
Sophia who?
Sophia the cat before dinner.

Knock, knock.
Who's there?
Kayley.
Kayley who?
Kayley on, it's just me.

Knock, knock.
Who's there?
Theresa.
Theresa who?
Theresa green until autumn.

Knock, knock.
Who's there?
Isobella.
Isobella who?
Isobella working, or should I knock again?

Knock, knock.
Who's there?
Avery.
Avery who?
Avery nice person. Open the door and see.

Knock, knock.
Who's there?
Gladys.
Gladys who?
I'm Gladys time for another knock-knock joke.

Knock, knock.
Who's there?
Sheri.
Sheri who?
I'll Sheri my secret if you open the door.

Knock, knock.
Who's there?
Kay.
Kay who?
Is it o-Kay if I tell another knock-knock joke?

Knock, knock.
Who's there?
Vanessa.
Vanessa who?
Vanessa door going to open?

Knock, knock.
Who's there?
Adelia.
Adelia who?
Adelia the cards and we'll
play Go Fish.

Knock, knock.
Who's there?
Lydia.
Lydia who?
The Lydia fell off the jam and made a big mess.

Knock, knock.
Who's there?
Robin.
Robin who?
Robin the pool but he can't swim.

Knock, knock.
Who's there?
Alberta.
Alberta who?
Alberta can't guess in a million years.

Knock, knock.
Who's there?
Elsie.
Elsie who?
Elsie if the back door is open.

Knock, knock.
Who's there?
Ella.
Ella who?
Why, don't you
look Ella-gant!

Knock, knock.
Who's there?
Penny.
Penny who?
Penny-guins live near the South Pole.

Knock, knock.
Who's there?
Alva.
Alva who?
Alva heart!

Knock, knock.
Who's there?
Irma.
Irma who?
Irma really hungry. Can I have a hot dog?

Knock, knock.
Who's there?
Aretha.
Aretha who?
Aretha flowers for you.

Knock, knock.
Who's there?
Eve.
Eve who?
I'll Eve you alone if you open the door.

Knock, knock.
Who's there?
Jess.
Jess who?
Jess me telling you a good knock-knock joke.

Knock, knock.
Who's there?
Bella.
Bella who?
Bella-nother knock-knock joke.

Health
Ha-Has

Knock, knock.

Who's there?

Two-thirty.

Two-thirty who?

I'm at the dentist because my two-thirty.

Knock, knock.
Who's there?
Hank R.
Hank R. who?
Please use a Hank-R.-chief when you sneeze!

Knock, knock.
Who's there?
Heart.
Heart who?
I'm having a heart time
opening the door.

Knock, knock.
Who's there?
Swatch.
Swatch who?
Bless you.

Knock, knock.
Who's there?
Colin.
Colin who?
Colin a doctor because I'm sick.

Knock, knock.
Who's there?
Blue.
Blue who?
Blue my nose since it was running.

Knock, knock.
Who's there?
Edith.
Edith who?
Edith. It'll make you feel better!

Knock, knock.
Who's there?
Ahhh.
Ahhh who?
Do you need a tissue?

Knock, knock.
Who's there?
Aida.
Aida who?
Aida lot of sweets and now
I've got a stomachache!

HATCH WHO!

Knock, knock.
Who's there?
Match.
Match who?
Gesundheit!

Knock, knock.
Who's there?
Eiffel.
Eiffel who?
Eiffel sick!

Knock, knock.
Who's there?
Eddy.
Eddy who?
Eddy idea how I can cure this cold?

Knock, knock.
Who's there?
Surgeon.
Surgeon who?
Surgeon you shall find.

Knock, knock.

Who's there?

Izzy.

Izzy who?

Izzy better with my glasses on.

Knock, knock.
Who's there?
Ophelia.
Ophelia who?
Ophelia pain. Headaches are the worst.

Knock, knock.
Who's there?
Bruce.
Bruce who?
I'll Bruce my knuckles if I keep knocking.

Knock, knock.
Who's there?
Pitcher.
Pitcher who?
Bless you! Are you catching a cold?

Household Humor

Knock, knock.
Who's there?
Colleen.
Colleen who?
Colleen up this mess before you leave.

Knock, knock.
Who's there?
House.
House who?
Hi, house are you doing?

Knock, knock.
Who's there?
Window.
Window who?
Window we get together again?

Knock, knock.
Who's there?
Hans R.
Hans R. who?
My Hans R. dirty. May I use your sink?

Knock, knock.
Who's there?
Spin.
Spin who?
You spin too much money on clothes.

Knock, knock.
Who's there?
Dragon.
Dragon who?
Dragon armchair over here and let's talk.

222

Knock, knock.

Who's there?

Figs.

Figs who?

Please figs the dishwasher—it's broken.

Knock, knock.

Who's there?

Hoof.

Hoof who?

Hoof to use the bathroom. Please let me in!

Knock, knock.
Who's there?
We.
We who?
It's time for a we-match.

Knock, knock.
Who's there?
Farmer.
Farmer who?
Farmer people live in houses than tents.

Knock, knock.
Who's there?
Garden.
Garden who?
A dog is garden its food dish in the kitchen.

Knock, knock.
Who's there?
Sasha.
Sasha who?
Took you Sasha long time to answer
the phone!

Knock, knock.
Who's there?
Howdy.
Howdy who?
Howdy cat get outside?

Knock, knock.
Who's there?
Wheel.
Wheel who?
Wheel be going out to dinner tonight.

Knock, knock.
Who's there?
Justin.
Justin who?
Justin the neighborhood. I thought I'd drop by.

Knock, knock.
Who's there?
Leash.
Leash who?
Leash you could do is open the door.

Knock, knock.
Who's there?
Luck.
Luck who?
Luck through the keyhole,
and you'll find out!

Knock, knock.
Who's there?
Scold.
Scold who?
Scold outside. May I come in?

Knock, knock.
Who's there?
Oil.
Oil who?
Oil be in the garage if you need me.

Knock, knock.
Who's there?
Samoa.
Samoa who?
Get Samoa food for the dog, please.

Knock, knock.
Who's there?
Hacienda.
Hacienda who?
Hacienda the story.

Knock, knock.
Who's there?
Moustache.
Moustache who?
I moustache you a question,
but I'll shave it for later.

Knock, knock.
Who's there?
Scott.
Scott who?
Scott a package for you. Open up!

Knock, knock.
Who's there?
Dishes.
Dishes who?
Dishes a nice place to visit!

Knock, knock.
Who's there?
Slam.
Slam who?
Slam-poo is in the shower.

Knock, knock.
Who's there?
Stopwatch.
Stopwatch who?
Stopwatch you're doing this instant!

Knock, knock.
Who's there?
Otter.
Otter who?
Otter you going to do in the basement?

Knock, knock.
Who's there?
Thermos.
Thermos who?
Thermos be someone home to let me in.

Knock, knock.
Who's there?
Switch.
Switch who?
Switch door should I use, front or back?

Knock, knock.
Who's there?
Reese.
Reese who?
Please Reese-cycle and save the planet.

Knock, knock.
Who's there?
Turnip.
Turnip who?
Turnip the volume. I can't hear the music!

Knock, knock.
Who's there?
Well water.
Well water who?
Well, water you waiting for? Open the door, please!

Knock, knock.
Who's there?
Icon.
Icon who?
Icon make you lunch if you are hungry.

Knock, knock.
Who's there?
Wire.
Wire who?
Wire you home? You should be at work!

Knock, knock.
Who's there?
Zany.
Zany who?
Zany-body seen the cat?

Knock, knock.
Who's there?
Philippa.
Philippa who?
Philippa bathtub—I'm covered in mud.

Knock, knock.
Who's there?
Needle.
Needle who?
Needle little money for the movies.

Knock, knock.
Who's there?
Musty.
Musty who?
Better get that musty pipe fixed!

Knock, knock.
Who's there?
Den.
Den who?
Den pigs fly.

Knock, knock.
Who's there?
Anne.
Anne who?
Want to go shopping for some Anne-tiques?

Knock, knock.
Who's there?
Otto.
Otto who?
Put your Otto-mobile in the garage.

Knock, knock.
Who's there?
Drake.
Drake who?
Can you Drake up
the leaves
out here?

Knock, knock.
Who's there?
Jimmy.
Jimmy who?
If you Jimmy a key, I can let myself in.

Knock, knock.
Who's there?
Sofa.
Sofa who?
Sofa these have been good knock-knock jokes.

Knock, knock.
Who's there?
Window.
Window who?
Window I get to hear some more knock-knock jokes?

Knock, knock.
Who's there?
Axel.
Axel who?
Axel lot of questions, get
a lot of answers.

Knock, knock.
Who's there?
Rufus.
Rufus who?
The Rufus on fire! Call 911!

Knock, knock.
Who's there?
Lois.
Lois who?
Look for the Lois price when
shopping for groceries.

Knock, knock.
Who's there?
Baby oil.
Baby oil who?
Baby oil will, and baby oil won't!

Knock, knock.
Who's there?
Alec.
Alec who?
Alec-tricity lights up my house.

Knock, knock.
Who's there?
CD.
CD who?
CD person on your doorstep?

Knock, knock.
Who's there?
Anita.
Anita who?
Anita bath. Please let me in!

Knock, knock.
Who's there?
Maya.
Maya who?
Maya bags are heavy—
can you help me carry them in?

Knock, knock.
Who's there?
Bed.
Bed who?
Bed over heels in love with you.

Knock, knock.

Who's there?

Bach.

Bach who?

Bach into the chicken coop!

Knock, knock.
Who's there?
Disco.
Disco who?
Disco-nnect the speaker.
The music is too loud.

Knock, knock.
Who's there?
Cymbals.
Cymbals who?
Cymbals have horns and others don't.

Knock, knock.
Who's there?
Ahmed.
Ahmed who?
Wolfgang Ahmed-eus Mozart!

Knock, knock.

Who's there?

Dishes.

Dishes who?

Dishes my favorite song. Turn it up!

Knock, knock.
Who's there?
Pig.
Pig who?
Pig a song, and we'll play along.

Knock, knock.
Who's there?
Cecil.
Cecil who?
Cecil have music wherever she goes.

Knock, knock.
Who's there?
Cheese.
Cheese who?
"Cheese a jolly good fellow!"

Knock, knock.

Who's there?

Parsley.

Parsley who?

Elvis Parsley played rock 'n' roll.

Knock, knock.

Who's there?

A mall.

A mall who?

A mall shook up!

Knock, knock.
Who's there?
Hubbard.
Hubbard who?
Hubbard can sing louder than my bird!

Knock, knock.
Who's there?
Ida.
Ida who?
Ida like to teach the world to sing!

Knock, knock.
Who's there?
Nadia.
Nadia who?
Nadia head while
the music plays!

Knock, knock.
Who's there?
Weevil.
Weevil who?
"Weevil, weevil ROCK YOU!"

Knock, knock.

Who's there?

Tuna.

Tuna who?

Tuna your banjo and you can be in our band.

Knock, knock.

Who's there?

Warrior.

Warrior who?

Warrior been? Rehearsal has started.

Knock, knock.

Who's there?

Mary Lee.

Mary Lee who?

"Mary Lee, Mary Lee,
life is but a dream. Row, row...."

Knock, knock.
Who's there?
Wicked.
Wicked who?
Wicked make beautiful music together.

Knock, knock.
Who's there?
Guitar.
Guitar who?
Guitar our coats.
We have to go.

Knock, knock.
Who's there?
Claire.
Claire who?
Claire-inet is one of the best wind instruments.

Knock, knock.
Who's there?
Bonnie.
Bonnie who?
My Bonnie lies over the ocean.

Knock, knock.
Who's there?
Chopin.
Chopin who?
Let's go Chopin for a new piano.

Knock, knock.
Who's there?
Mike.
Mike who?
Sing into the
Mike-rophone, please.

Knock, knock.
Who's there?
Tuba.
Tuba who?
Tuba toothpaste is empty—
I can't brush my teeth.

Knock, knock.
Who's there?
Harmony.
Harmony who?
Harmony knock-knock jokes
do you know?

Knock, knock.
Who's there?
Ringo.
Ringo who?
"Ringo round the rosie!"

Knock, knock.

Who's there?

Yam.

Yam who?

The yam session is groovy.

Out-Of-
This-
World
Jokes

Knock, knock.
Who's there?
Destroyed.
Destroyed who?
Destroyed came this close
to the planet!

Knock, knock.
Who's there?
Launch.
Launch who?
Launch is served, come eat!

Knock, knock.
Who's there?
Dee.
Dee who?
Dee planets revolve around Dee sun.

Knock, knock.
Who's there?
UFO.
UFO who?
UFO me three dollars.

Knock, knock.
Who's there?
Comet.
Comet who?
Comet open this door, please!

Knock, knock.
Who's there?
Meteor.
Meteor who?
Meteor burgers are the best kind.

Knock, knock.
Who's there?
Planet.
Planet who?
Planet and the rocket launch will happen.

Knock, knock.
Who's there?
Rocket.
Rocket who?
Rocket any more, and
the boat will tip over!

Knock, knock.
Who's there?
Saturn.
Saturn who?
Saturn-ly, the door opened wide!

Knock, knock.
Who's there?
Wok.
Wok who?
The moon-wok is
an astronaut's favorite dance.

Knock, knock.
Who's there?
Delight.
Delight who?
Delight of the Moon is lovely.

Knock, knock.
Who's there?
Quasar.
Quasar who?
Quasar-dillas sound good for lunch!

Knock, knock.
Who's there?
Mars.
Mars who?
Dancing with the Mars is my favorite show.

Knock, knock.
Who's there?
Apollo.
Apollo who?
I Apollo-gize for blasting
off early.

Knock, knock.
Who's there?
Universe.
Universe who?
Universe-ities are important for astronauts.

Knock, knock.
Who's there?
Moon.
Moon who?
Moon-day is the hardest day of the week.

Knock, knock.
Who's there?
Neptune.
Neptune who?
Neptunes sound out of this world.

Knock, knock.
Who's there?
Snail.
Snail who?
Snail-iens are the slowest aliens.

Knock, knock.
Who's there?
Eclipse.
Eclipse who?
Eclipse my hair, and I pay him.

Knock, knock.
Who's there?
Alien.
Alien who?
Just how many aliens do you know?

Knock, knock.
Who's there?
Martha.
Martha who?
Martha-matics books are filled with problems.

Knock, knock.
Who's there?
Ed.
Ed who?
Education is important for everyone.

Knock, knock.
Who's there?
Ice.
Ice who?
Ice-osceles triangles are
the coldest shape.

Knock, knock.
Who's there?
Zeroes.
Zeroes who?
Zeroes as fast as she can, but she still loses her boat race.

Knock, knock.
Who's there?
Wayne.
Wayne who?
Sit Wayne front if you want to see the board.

Knock, knock.
Who's there?
Math.
Math who?
Math potatoes and gravy is my favorite food.

Knock, knock.
Who's there?
Broken pencil.
Broken pencil who?
Forget it. It's pointless.

Knock, knock.
Who's there?
Canoe.
Canoe who?
Canoe help me with my homework?

Knock, knock.
Who's there?
Geometry.
Geometry who?
Geometry in the school play, but I wish I was a flower.

Knock, knock.
Who's there?
Jamaica.
Jamaica who?
Jamaica good grade on your math test?

Knock, knock.
Who's there?
Norma Lee.
Norma Lee who?
Norma Lee I'd be in school now, but I have the day off.

Knock, knock.
Who's there?
Pasture.
Pasture who?
Pasture homework in, please.

Knock, knock.
Who's there?
Polly.
Polly who?
Polly-nomial. Why the third degree?

Knock, knock.
Who's there?
Rich.
Rich who?
Rich subject is your favorite?

Knock, knock.
Who's there?
Sahara.
Sahara who?
Sahara you doing in school?

Knock, knock.
Who's there?
Rhino.
Rhino who?
Rhino everything to graduate.

Knock, knock.

Who's there?

Thumb.

Thumb who?

Thumb dog ate my homework!

Knock, knock.
Who's there?
To.
To who?
No! It's *to whom.*

Knock, knock.
Who's there?
Wafer.
Wafer who?
Wafer the bus at the corner.

Knock, knock.

Who's there?

Winner.

Winner who?

Winner you going to finish your homework?

Knock, knock.

Who's there?

Z.

Z who?

Z you at school tomorrow!

Knock, knock.
Who's there?
Ahmed.
Ahmed who?
Ahmed a mistake. Give me an eraser.

Knock, knock.
Who's there?
Web.
Web who?
Web-ster's Dictionary is the best
place to learn definitions.

Knock, knock.
Who's there?
Anita.
Anita who?
Anita borrow a pencil!

Knock, knock.
Who's there?
Betsy.
Betsy who?
Betsy of all, school's almost over.

Knock, knock.
Who's there?
Door.
Door who?
Door your homework!

Knock, knock.
Who's there?
Orange.
Orange who?
Orange you glad we are out of school?

Knock, knock.
Who's there?
Schnauzer.
Schnauzer who?
Schnauzer homework coming?

Knock, knock.
Who's there?
Sty.
Sty who?
Sty home from school if you feel ill.

Knock, knock.
Who's there?
Warner.
Warner who?
Warner ride to school?

Knock, knock.
Who's there?
Misty.
Misty who?
Misty bus. I'm going to be late!

Knock, knock.

Who's there?

Paige.

Paige who?

This book is a real Paige-turner.

Knock, knock.
Who's there?
Nova.
Nova who?
Nova-cation during summer school.

Knock, knock.
Who's there?
Paulie.
Paulie who?
Paulie-gons are my favorite shape.

Knock, knock.
Who's there?
Mark.
Mark who?
Use a Mark-er. I'll use crayons.

Knock, knock.
Who's there?
Wordy.
Wordy who?
Wordy math questions easy,
or was it just me?

Knock, knock.
Who's there?
Cole.
Cole who?
Cole-ege is coming soon, so you better work hard.

Knock, knock.
Who's there?
Ada.
Ada who?
You have to Ada lot of numbers
to get a million!

Knock, knock.
Who's there?
Karen and Sharon.
Karen and Sharon who?
Karen and Sharon are things all friends should do.

Knock, knock.
Who's there?
Megan.
Megan who?
Stop Megan marks on my paper!

Knock, knock.

Who's there?

Mike.

Mike who?

Mike-rayons are getting too short to use.

Knock, knock.

Who's there?

Meal.

Meal who?

Meal late—I'll miss the bus!

Knock, knock.
Who's there?
Warren.
Warren who?
Warren you in this same class last year?

Knock, knock.
Who's there?
Tents.
Tents who?
Please don't give me de-tents-ion!

Knock, knock.
Who's there?
Annie.
Annie who?
"Annie-thing you can do, I can do better!"

Knock, knock.
Who's there?
Bond.
Bond who?
You're bond to get it if you keep trying!

Knock, knock.
Who's there?
Gladys.
Gladys who?
Gladys the weekend. No homework!

Knock, knock.
Who's there?
Tangents.
Tangents who?
Tangents like to spend a lot of time on the beach.

Knock, knock.
Who's there?
Ohms.
Ohms who?
Sherlock Ohms at your service. . . .

Knock, knock.
Who's there?
Saturn.
Saturn who?
I Saturn my phone and the glass cracked.

Knock, knock.
Who's there?
Alkynes.
Alkynes who?
Alkynes of ways to open the door, so please do.

Knock, knock.
Who's there?
Pi.
Pi who?
Three-point-one-four-one-five-nine-two . . .

Knock, knock.
Who's there?
Owl.
Owl who?
Owl-gebra.

Knock, knock.
Who's there?
One plus one.
One plus one who?
Yes, one plus one is two.

Knock, knock.
Who's there?
Hard drive.
Hard drive who?
I had a hard drive. Let me in so I can relax.

Knock, knock.
Who's there?
C.
C *who?*
C you at school!

Knock, knock.
Who's there?
Ewe.
Ewe who?
Ewe are my favorite teacher!

Knock, knock.
Who's there?
Vivaldi.
Vivaldi who?
Vivaldi books, I feel like I'm drowning.

Knock, knock.
Who's there?
Perez.
Perez who?
I want to be Perez-ident when I grow up.

Knock, knock.
Who's there?
Teacher.
Teacher who?
Teacher to go knocking on my door
in the middle of the night!

Knock, knock.
Who's there?
Ape.
Ape who?
"Ape, B, C, D . . ."

Knock, knock.
Who's there?
Wayne.
Wayne who?
Wayne is our homework due?

281

Knock, knock.
Who's there?
B-2.
B-2 who?
B-2 school on time!

Knock, knock.
Who's there?
Double.
Double who?
W!

Knock, knock.
Who's there?
Two 4s.
Two 4s who?
Two 4s can skip lunch because they're already 8.

Knock, knock.
Who's there?
Mode.
Mode who?
I mode your lawn. You owe me $10.

Knock, knock.
Who's there?
Weirdo.
Weirdo who?
Weirdo we go for recess today?

Knock, knock.
Who's there?
Math.
Math who?
Math-letes love to keep score.

Side-Splitting Sports

Knock, knock.
Who's there?
Run.
Run who?
Getting there is half the run.

Knock, knock.
Who's there?
Hi.
Hi who?
Hi-yah! I'm getting good at karate!

Knock, knock.
Who's there?
Money.
Money who?
Money hurts when I run.

Knock, knock.
Who's there?
Tennis.
Tennis who?
Tennis eight plus two.

Knock, knock.
Who's there?
Love.
Love who?
Love-40. You are winning the tennis match!

Knock, knock.
Who's there?
Tiger.
Tiger who?
Tiger before she gets to first base.

Knock, knock.
Who's there?
Adolph.
Adolph who?
Adolph ball hit me in the mouth!

Knock, knock.
Who's there?
Rene.
Rene who?
Rene the marathon!

Knock, knock.
Who's there?
Hockey.
Hockey who?
Hockey doesn't work, so I had to knock.

Knock, knock.
Who's there?
Almond.
Almond who?
Not almond like watching football.

Knock, knock.

Who's there?

Annette.

Annette who?

Annette catches more fish than a hook.

Knock, knock.

Who's there?

Isabelle.

Isabelle who?

Isabelle necessary on a bicycle?

Knock, knock.
Who's there?
Pasta.
Pasta who?
Pasta ball—I'm open!

Knock, knock.
Who's there?
Paul.
Paul who?
Paul up the anchor, and let's go!

Knock, knock.
Who's there?
Andy.
Andy who?
Andy winner is . . .

Knock, knock.
Who's there?
Otto.
Otto who?
Otto breath from
running the mile.

Knock, knock.
Who's there?
Fumble.
Fumble who?
Fumble-bees are the clumsiest insects.

Knock, knock.
Who's there?
Dozen.
Dozen who?
Dozen anyone in this town play football?

Knock, knock.
Who's there?
Les.
Les who?
Les go and play golf!

Knock, knock.
Who's there?
Harvey.
Harvey who?
Harvey gonna play this game forever?

Knock, knock.
Who's there?
Sock.
Sock who?
Sock-er is my favorite sport.

Knock, knock.
Who's there?
Tahiti.
Tahiti who?
Tahiti home run, you have to be a swinger.

Knock, knock.
Who's there?
Kelp.
Kelp who?
Kelp me. I can't swim!

Knock, knock.
Who's there?
Jim.
Jim who?
Jim-nasts need to have great balance.

Knock, knock.
Who's there?
Duncan.
Duncan who?
Duncan score—I win.

Knock, knock.
Who's there?
Clem.
Clem who?
Clem-ing a mountain takes perseverance!

Knock, knock.

Who's there?

Kent.

Kent who?

I Kent blink, or I'll lose the staring contest.

Knock, knock.

Who's there?

Bass.

Bass who?

Bass-ball is my favorite sport.

Knock, knock.

Who's there?

Rowan.

Rowan who?

Better start Rowan if you want to win the race.

Knock, knock.
Who's there?
Discuss.
Discuss who?
Discuss is my favorite track event.

Knock, knock.
Who's there?
Judo.
Judo who?
Judo-n't stand a chance
against our team.

Knock, knock.

Who's there?

Juan.

Juan who?

Juan-on-one, I can beat you at basketball.

Knock, knock.

Who's there?

New Jersey.

New Jersey who?

We need a New Jersey for the quarterback—his is torn.

Knock, knock.

Who's there?

Boat.

Boat who?

Boat time to start the race!

Knock, knock.
Who's there?
Indie.
Indie who?
Kick the ball Indie net to score.

Knock, knock.
Who's there?
Bleat.
Bleat who?
The bleat-chers were full of cheering goat fans.

Knock, knock.
Who's there?
Lou.
Lou who?
Lou-sing games can be hard.

Knock, knock.
Who's there?
Thyme.
Thyme who?
You're just in thyme to play a game with us.

Knock, knock.
Who's there?
Stripes.
Stripes who?
Three stripes, you're out!

Knock, knock.

Who's there?

Banana.

Banana who?

Banana-sters are fun to slide down.

Knock, knock.
Who's there?
Roo.
Roo who?
Roo would know if you opened the door.

Knock, knock.
Who's there?
Hugo.
Hugo who?
Hugo first. It's too dark out there.

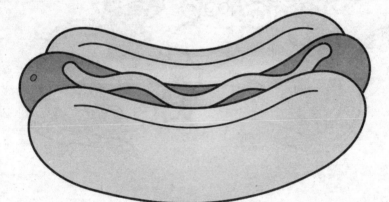

Knock, knock.
Who's there?
Irish.
Irish who?
"Irish I were an Oscar Mayer wiener!"

Knock, knock.
Who's there?
Stew.
Stew who?
Stew-ing good!

Knock, knock.
Who's there?
Eilleen.
Eilleen who?
Eilleen-ed over and fell into the pool!

Knock, knock.
Who's there?
Wire.
Wire who?
Wire you asking?

Knock, knock.
Who's there?
Dill.
Dill who?
Dill me in. I'd like to play.

Knock, knock.
Who's there?
Cotton.
Cotton who?
Cotton a trap. Can you help me out?

Knock, knock.
Who's there?
Clothes.
Clothes who?
That was a clothes call!

Knock, knock.
Who's there?
Two shoes.
Two shoes who?
Two shoes please, I'm about to sneeze.

Knock, knock.
Who's there?
Miso.
Miso who?
Miso happy to see you!

Knock, knock.

Who's there?
Toupees.
Toupees who?
Toupees in a pod.

Knock, knock.
Who's there?
Avenue.
Avenue who?
Avenue been missing me?

Knock, knock.
Who's there?
Cargo.
Cargo who?
Cargo *beep, beep!*

Knock, knock.
Who's there?
Miss Terry.
Miss Terry who?
It's a Miss Terry. Open the door to find out.

Knock, knock.
Who's there?
Castle.
Castle who?
You castle lot of questions, don't you?

Knock, knock.
Who's there?
Dozen.
Dozen who?
Dozen anyone want to
let me in?

Knock, knock.
Who's there?
Ears.
Ears who?
Ears another knock-knock joke!

Knock, knock.
Who's there?
Lab.
Lab who?
Labracadabra!

Knock, knock.
Who's there?
Waiter.
Waiter who?
Waiter minute while I take this call.

Knock, knock.
Who's there?
Fairy.
Fairy who?
Fairy pleased to meet you!

Knock, knock.
Who's there?
Fantasy.
Fantasy who?
Fantasy-ing you here!

Knock, knock.
Who's there?
Ha-ha-ho.
Ha-ha-ho who?
I'm laughing because I saw the jokes that are coming up.

Knock, knock.
Who's there?
Howl.
Howl who?
Howl I know there's not a monster under my bed?

Knock, knock.
Who's there?
I'm.
I'm who?
Don't you know who you are?

Knock, knock.
Who's there?
Justice.
Justice who?
Justice once, can you let me in?

Knock, knock.
Who's there?
Knights.
Knights who?
Knights to meet you!

Knock, knock.
Who's there?
Earwig.
Earwig who?
Earwig go again.

Knock, knock.
Who's there?
Mew.
Mew who?
Let's go to the mew-seum today.

Knock, knock.
Who's there?
Ogre.
Ogre who?
I'm ogre here! Come find me.

Knock, knock.
Who's there?
Bea.
Bea who?
Bea-fore you leave, let me tell you something.

Knock, knock.
Who's there?
Police.
Police who?
Police pass the salt.

Knock, knock.
Who's there?
Glow.
Glow who?
You glow, girl!

Knock, knock.
Who's there?
Slug.
Slug who?
Slug-y to find a four-leaf clover.

Knock, knock.
Who's there?
Hans.
Hans who?
Hans off the steering wheel. I am driving.

Knock, knock.
Who's there?
Sonata.
Sonata who?
Sonata big deal, I just
wanted to say *hello*.

Knock, knock.
Who's there?
Voodoo.
Voodoo who?
Voodoo you think it is?

Knock, knock.
Who's there?
Statue.
Statue who?
It's me. Statue?

Knock, knock.
Who's there?
Tank.
Tank who?
Tank you for being
my friend!

Knock, knock.
Who's there?
Whom.
Whom who?
I just wanted to see if you were whom.

Knock, knock.
Who's there?
Thistle.
Thistle who?
Thistle only take a minute, I promise!

Knock, knock.
Who's there?
Eerie.
Eerie who?
Eerie is! Happy to see you!

Knock, knock.
Who's there?
Thrush.
Thrush who?
What's thrush? We have plenty of time.

Knock, knock.
Who's there?
'Tis.
'Tis who?
'Tis who is good to wipe
your nose.

Knock, knock.
Who's there?
Penne.
Penne who?
Penne for your thoughts.

Knock, knock.
Who's there?
Wool.
Wool who?
Wool you go bowling with me?

Knock, knock.
Who's there?
Tooth.
Tooth who?
Tooth or dare?

Knock, knock.

Who's there?

Tree.

Tree who?

I'll give you tree guesses.

Knock, knock.

Who's there?

Pika.

Pika who?

Pika card, any card.

Knock, knock.
Who's there?
Trot.
Trot who?
Trot you would like some company.

Knock, knock.
Who's there?
Tummy.
Tummy who?
Tummy your name, and I'll tell you mine.

Knock, knock.
Who's there?
Sour.
Sour who?
Sour your friends doing these days?

Knock, knock.
Who's there?
Mister.
Mister who?
Mister last bus home.

Knock, knock.
Who's there?
Warrior.
Warrior who?
Warrior been? I've been knocking and knocking!

Knock, knock.
Who's there?
Buddy.
Buddy who?
Some-buddy who wants
to be your friend.

Knock, knock.
Who's there?
Who.
Who who?
There's a terrible echo in here, isn't there?

Knock, knock.
Who's there?
Tanks.
Tanks who?
Tanks for all the laughs!

Knock, knock.
Who's there?
Carson.
Carson who?
Carson roads can be dangerous, so use the crosswalk.

Knock, knock.
Who's there?
Sid.
Sid who?
Sid down and tell me a story.

Knock, knock.
Who's there?
Yeast.
Yeast who?
Yeast you could do is come say *hi.*

Knock, knock.
Who's there?
Wooden shoe.
Wooden shoe who?
Wooden shoe like to go to
the movies with me?

Knock, knock.
Who's there?
Yee.
Yee who?
What are you? A cowboy?

Knock, knock.
Who's there?
Yule log.
Yule log who?
Yule log the door after you let me in, right?

Knock, knock.
Who's there?
Toodle.
Toodle who?
Toodle-oo to you, too!

Knock, knock.
Who's there?
Yellow.
Yellow who?
Yellow there!

Knock, knock.
Who's there?
Pastor.
Pastor who?
Pastor mashed potatoes, please.

Knock, knock.
Who's there?
White.
White who?
I'm white here, can't you hear me?

Knock, knock.
Who's there?
Adair.
Adair who?
Adair you to do it again!

Knock, knock.
Who's there?
Fire.
Fire who?
Fire you waiting to let me in?

Knock, knock.
Who's there?
Burglar.
Burglar who?
Burglars don't knock.

Will you remember me in an hour?
Yes.
Will you remember me in a day?
Yes.
Will you remember me in a week?
Yes.
Will you remember me in a month?
Yes.
Will you remember me in a year?
Yes.
I think you won't.
Yes I will.
Knock, knock.
Who's there?
See—you've forgotten me already.

Knock, knock.
Who's there?
Wedge.
Wedge who?
Wedge you go? I've been
looking for you!

323

Knock, knock.
Who's there?
Nobody.
Nobody who?
(Stay silent)

Knock, knock.
Who's there?
Cook.
Cook who?
Who are you calling cuckoo?

Knock, knock.
Who's there?
Déjà.
Déjà who?
Knock, knock.

Knock, knock.
Who's there?
General Lee.
General Lee who?
General Lee, I knock and you open the door.

Knock, knock.
Who's there?
Iona Carr.
Iona Carr who?
Iona Carr—do you need a ride?

Knock, knock.
Who's there?
Viper.
Viper who?
Viper the window so you can see!

Knock, knock.
Who's there?
Orson.
Orson who?
Who uses an Orson cart to
get around anymore?

Knock, knock.
Who's there?
Anita.
Anita who?
I sent you mail—Anita letter back!

Knock, knock.
Who's there?
Loading.
Loading who?
I hear you loading clear. Now open the door.

Knock, knock.
Who's there?
Wood.
Wood who?
Wood you please let me in?

Knock, knock.
Who's there?
Armageddon.
Armageddon who?
Armageddon a little bored. Let's get out of here.

Knock, knock.

Who's there?

Stan.

Stan who?

Stan up so I can see you.

Knock, knock.

Who's there?

Toby.

Toby who?

Toby better at anything, you have to practice.

Knock, knock.
Who's there?
Artichokes.
Artichokes who?
Artichokes on his food
if he eats too quickly.

Knock, knock.
Who's there?
Leaf.
Leaf who?
I won't leaf, so let me in.

Knock, knock.
Who's there?
Jewel.
Jewel who?
Jewel have to let me in soon.

Knock, knock.
Who's there?
Dan Wright.
Dan Wright who?
Look left Dan Wright when crossing
the street.

Knock, knock.
Who's there?
Sandy.
Sandy who?
Sandy wood, and then I'll paint it.

Knock, knock.
Who's there?
Land.
Land who?
No, land ho!

Knock, knock.
Who's there?
Carrot.
Carrot who?
Don't you carrot all that I'm out here knocking?

Knock, knock.
Who's there?
Handsome.
Handsome who?
Handsome food to me. I'm hungry!

Knock, knock.
Who's there?
Frank.
Frank who?
Can I be Frank? I really want you to open this door!

Knock, knock.
Who's there?
Elba.
Elba who?
Elba happy to tell you another
knock-knock joke.

Knock, knock.
Who's there?
Zany.
Zany who?
Zany-body want to play video games?

Knock, knock.
Who's there?
Sore.
Sore who?
Sore-y, I think I'm knocking on the wrong door.

Knock, knock.
Who's there?
Acorn.
Acorn who?
Acorn-y joke!

Knock, knock.
Who's there?
Rudy.
Rudy who?
It's Rudy to never say *please*
or *thank you*.

Knock, knock.
Who's there?
Police.
Police who?
Police come out and play with me.

Knock, knock.
Who's there?
Sum.
Sum who?
Sum-thing's gotta give!

Knock, knock.
Who's there?
Pauline.
Pauline who?
I think I'm Pauline in love with you.

Knock, knock.
Who's there?
Sincerely.
Sincerely who?
Sincerely this morning, I've been
waiting for you to answer.

Knock, knock.
Who's there?
Arfur.
Arfur who?
Arfur got!

Knock, knock.
Who's there?
Wire.
Wire who?
Wire you always asking *who's there?*

Knock, knock.
Who's there?
Monk.
Monk who?
Monkey see, monkey do!

Knock, knock.
Who's there?
Avenue.
Avenue who?
Avenue seen me coming?

Knock, knock.
Who's there?
FBI.
FBI who?
We're asking the questions here.

Knock, knock.
Who's there?
Ivor.
Ivor who?
Ivor you open the door or I'll climb in the window.

Knock, knock.
Who's there?
Watt.
Watt who?
Watt do you want from me?

Knock, knock.
Who's there?
Iguana.
Iguana who?
Iguana be your best friend.

Knock, knock.
Who's there?
Algo.
Algo who?
Algo anywhere with you.

Knock, knock.
Who's there?
Iris.
Iris who?
Iris you were here.

Knock, knock.
Who's there?
Fran.
Fran who?
Fran-dship is a great thing.

Knock, knock.
Who's there?
Amish.
Amish who?
Really, you're a shoe? Pee-yew!

Wacky Weather

Knock, knock.
Who's there?
Snow.
Snow who?
Snow way I'm telling you.

Knock, knock.
Who's there?
Wayne.
Wayne who?
Wayne drops keep falling on my head!

Knock, knock.
Who's there?
Icy.
Icy who?
Icy you!

Knock, knock.
Who's there?
Drought.
Drought who?
I drought you remembered to shut the windows.

Knock, knock.
Who's there?
Reindeer.
Reindeer who?
It's starting to reindeer.

Knock, knock.
Who's there?
Stun.
Stun who?
Stun-shiny days are great
days for the beach.

Knock, knock.

Who's there?

Weed.

Weed who?

Weed better go. There's a storm coming.

Knock, knock.
Who's there?
Accordion.
Accordion who?
Accordion to the forecast, it's going to snow tomorrow!

Knock, knock.
Who's there?
Butter.
Butter who?
Butter bring an umbrella. It looks like it might rain!

Knock, knock.
Who's there?
Cloud.
Cloud who?
Two's company, three's a cloud.

Knock, knock.
Who's there?
Emma.
Emma who?
Emma bit cold out here—let me in!

Knock, knock.
Who's there?
Hoover.
Hoover who?
Hoover the rainbow!

Knock, knock.
Who's there?
Snow says.
Snow says who?
Snow says nothing—
it can't talk!

Knock, knock.
Who's there?
Ina Claire.
Ina Claire who?
Ina Claire day, you can see for miles!

Knock, knock.
Who's there?
Mist.
Mist who?
Mist seeing the rainbow.

Knock, knock.
Who's there?
Weather.
Weather who?
Weather smoke, there's fire.

Knock, knock.
Who's there?
Hurricane.
Hurricane who?
Hurricane you run away from the storm?

Knock, knock.
Who's there?
Wendy.
Wendy who?
It's Wendy today and cloudy tomorrow.

Knock, knock.
Who's there?
Icicle.
Icicle who?
Icicle to the store and get some milk.

Knock, knock.
Who's there?
Proud.
Proud who?
Proud me out—I'm getting snowed in!

Knock, knock.
Who's there?
Ray.
Ray who?
Ray-ny days are good for playing inside.

Knock, knock.

Who's there?

Twist.

Twist who?

Twister is a tornado's favorite game.

Knock, knock.
Who's there?
Gus T.
Gus T. who?
This wind is really Gus T.

Knock, knock.
Who's there?
Al.
Al who?
I'm Al wet in the rain.

Knock, knock.
Who's there?
Zeke.
Zeke who?
Zeke shelter. A storm is coming.

Knock, knock.
Who's there?
Ichabod.
Ichabod who?
Ichabod storm out. Can I borrow an umbrella?

Knock, knock.
Who's there?
Indy.
Indy who?
Want to play Indy snow?

Knock, knock.
Who's there?
Dewy.
Dewy who?
Dewy have to go soon?

Knock, knock.
Who's there?
Summer.
Summer who?
Summer hot and summer cold.

Knock, knock.
Who's there?
Snow.
Snow who?
Snow laughing matter.

Knock, knock.
Who's there?
Fowl.
Fowl who?
Fowl weather ruins our fun.

Knock, knock.
Who's there?
Poodle.
Poodle who?
Poodles happen after it rains.

Knock, knock.
Who's there?
Frostbite.
Frostbite who?
Frostbite your food, then chew and swallow.

Knock, knock.
Who's there?
Drizzle.
Drizzle who?
Drizzle-y bears love to play in the rain.

Knock, knock.
Who's there?
August.
August who?
August of wind might blow you over.

Knock, knock.
Who's there?
Heat.
Heat who?
"Pleased to heat you," said the Sun to Earth.